THE RETURN OF FOOD: POVERTY AND URBAN FOOD SECURITY IN ZIMBABWE AFTER THE CRISIS

GODFREY TAWODZERA, LIAM RILEY
AND JONATHAN CRUSH

SERIES EDITOR: PROF. JONATHAN CRUSH

AFSUN

© AFSUN 2016

Published by the African Food Security Urban Network (AFSUN)
African Centre for Cities, University of Cape Town, Private Bag X3
Rondebosch 7701, South Africa and Balsillie School of International
Affairs, Waterloo, Canada
www.afsun.org

First published 2016

ISBN 978-1-920597-14-6

Cover photo: Zimbabwean street vendors march towards Parliament to
submit a petition appealing the eviction of vendors from the streets during
a protest on June 24, 2015 in Harare (AFP Photo/Jekesai Njikizana)

Production by Bronwen Dachs Muller, Cape Town

Printed by MegaDigital, Cape Town

AUTHORS

Godfrey Tawodzera is a Senior Lecturer, Department of Geography and Environmental Sciences, University of Limpopo, Polokwane, South Africa.

Liam Riley is an SSHRC Post-Doctoral Fellow at the Balsillie School of International Affairs, Waterloo, Canada.

Jonathan Crush is CIGI Chair in Global Migration and Development, Balsillie School of International Affairs, and Honorary Professor at the University of Cape Town.

Previous Publications in the AFSUN Series

CONTENTS

TABLES

FIGURES

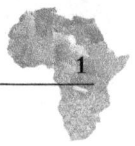

1. INTRODUCTION

> Food stores are filled to the brim with groceries, but most of us here are jobless and therefore have no money to consistently buy very basic foodstuffs, resulting in us having mostly one meal per day (Josphat Madyira, 2015).[1]

For two decades Zimbabwe has suffered a profound political, economic and social malaise. Although the country was a net exporter of food in the 1980s and early 1990s, after 2000 it became a net food importer and a major recipient of food aid.[2] These years were also characterized by a negative GDP growth rate, rising unemployment, increasing poverty, hyperinflation, mass out-migration and recurrent national food shortages.[3] Most households in the country struggled to meet their food needs. While both rural and urban households were subjected to this turbulent environment, the challenges for households in the city, particularly the poor, were acute given the massive job losses resulting from economic decline, increases in the cost of housing, water, electricity and transportation, and hyperinflation.[4] The causes of the crisis have been widely debated but there is consensus that it reached its nadir in 2008.[5] GDP had contracted by over 40% between 2000 and 2006; annual inflation increased from two-digit figures in 2000 to 231 million percent in July 2008 and the country's external debt ballooned to USD6 billion in 2008.[6] Life expectancy, which had peaked at 61 years in 1990, fell to around 36 years in 2008. That year, political violence and the accumulation of failed economic policies contributed to a drop in food production and a halt to imports, which created a humanitarian emergency that affected millions of households in Zimbabwe. The country received USD490 million in humanitarian aid in 2008, while its foreign currency reserves stood at only USD6 million.

To understand the scope of the food security challenge that confronted households in Zimbabwe during the crisis, it is necessary to recall the broader economic and political context created by the country's Economic Structural Adjustment Programme (ESAP), the Fast Track Land Reform Programme (FTLRP) and Operation Murambatsvina (Restore Order). All of these politically-inspired developments played a role in undermining urban livelihoods and increasing household food insecurity.[7] ESAP laid the foundation for the serious downward trajectory in the Zimbabwean economy in the late 1990s and 2000s.[8] The programme was introduced in Zimbabwe in 1991 when the country's post-independence economic growth was slowing, foreign investment was declining, and unemployment was increasing. ESAP was meant to revamp the economy,

encourage investment and reduce the country's domestic and international debt through a three-pronged strategy of trade liberalization, domestic deregulation and investment promotion, and fiscal and monetary policies to curtail state expenditure. In practice, these austerity measures led to the closure of many factories, large-scale retrenchments, declining real wages, skyrocketing consumer prices, and a decline in the formal economy.[9]

Another critical development with direct food security implications was the launch of the government's land reform programme in 2000. The FTLRP aimed to expropriate the country's white-owned farms and redistribute them to indigenous black farmers. By the end of 2002, only 600 of 4,500 white farmers were still in the country.[10] Although over 1.2 million black farmers benefitted from the FTLRP, national agricultural production drastically declined as the new occupants lacked the financial resources, inputs, labour, equipment and expertise to produce on the same scale. As a result, the country quickly changed from being a net exporter to a net importer of food. Maize production deficits averaged over 500,000 tonnes per annum after 2000. While production levels improved somewhat in the newly resettled areas after 2004, they did not offset the losses incurred by the termination of white commercial agriculture. From its inception, the programme greatly increased food insecurity in the country. In urban areas, the impact was particularly negative as very little food filtered into towns and cities from the rural areas to feed those already reeling under the general macro-economic meltdown.

In 2005, the government launched an assault on all forms of urban informality, including the informal food economy. Operation Murambatsvina destroyed backyard houses, vending stalls, flea markets and informal businesses in many cities.[11] Although the motives behind the campaign are disputed (with some seeing it as a politically-motivated attack on opposition strongholds in the urban areas), there is no denying that it caused massive disruption of livelihoods and destruction of urban housing. Many income-generating projects were destroyed and more than 700,000 urbanites lost their homes, jobs and livelihoods. Operation Garikayi, launched in the aftermath of Operation Murambatsvina to construct houses for some of the affected families, failed to mitigate the negative impacts as the government had neither the capacity nor the resources to ensure meaningful reparations. Operation Murambatsvina rearranged Zimbabwe's urban landscape and worsened the plight of the urban poor, increasing their vulnerability to hunger and food insecurity.

The impacts of these policies were exacerbated by serious economic mismanagement. As one commentator noted: "Ill-conceived macroeconomic policies superimposed on counterproductive trade and industrial

policies joined with a crisis and the worst global recession since the 1930s to hurl Zimbabwe into the recessionary jaws of hyperinflation. The lack of sound economic policies and the failure to service past debt meant that access to foreign borrowing was lost."[12] By 2008, the food situation in Zimbabwe was dire. The International Federation of Red Cross and Red Crescent Societies estimated that about 5.1 million of the country's 11.6 people would have no access to food by the end of that year. The government was constrained from importing food by inadequate funding and rampant inflation. From April to October 2008, both the government and humanitarian agencies managed to import a total of only 316,000 metric tonnes of cereals, leaving the cereal harvest deficit for 2008/2009 at 666,000 metric tonnes. Although the government indicated that it would import 600,000 tonnes of maize from South Africa, only 175,000 metric tonnes had been imported by the end of August 2008.

For most of 2008, the market was characterized by constant staple food shortages. The formal food system virtually collapsed and most foodstuffs could only be accessed on the parallel market. The situation was particularly grave in urban areas where households had to purchase most of their food. Further aggravating the economic crisis was political uncertainty resulting from the disputed 2008 election. Harmonized elections for municipal, parliamentary and presidential positions were held in March 2008, but disputes surrounding the outcome of the presidential election, and the subsequent run-off poll that was boycotted by the opposition, created a volatile atmosphere in the country.

The 2008 crisis coincided with the implementation of a baseline household food security survey by AFSUN in low-income areas of 11 Southern African cities including Harare. Among the 462 households surveyed in Harare, rates of formal unemployment and food poverty were extremely high. Almost all were food insecure (96%) and nearly three-quarters (72%) were severely food insecure.[13] Dietary diversity was lower than in any other city in Southern Africa. Indeed, households in low-income urban areas in Harare were far worse off in terms of all the food insecurity and poverty indicators than households in the other 10 Southern African cities surveyed by AFSUN.

After 2008, Zimbabwe's political and economic situation stabilized somewhat. During the eight months following the election run-off, for example, the ruling party and the opposition negotiated the terms of a power-sharing agreement. The resulting Government of National Unity was inaugurated in February 2009 and was to last until 2013. The formation of this coalition government and the abandonment of the Zimbabwean dollar helped to stabilize the economy, arresting the precipitous

decline in GDP, bringing down inflation, introducing a multi-currency regime and improving the food supply.[14] Between 2009 and 2011, Zimbabwe's GDP growth averaged 7.3%, making it one of the world's fastest growing economies, albeit from a very low base. According to the World Bank, Zimbabwe experienced an economic rebound after 2009 "and with the support of record international price levels, exports of minerals - notably diamonds, platinum, gold, and other products - have injected new life into the economy."[15] Zimbabwean trade flows rebounded with exports rising at 39% per year. Imports also rose quickly, averaging 34% per year from 2009 to 2011, in response to domestic demand. However, mining accounted for a significant proportion of export growth, constituting 50% of total exports during the period 2010-2012,[16] and the growing reliance of the economy on mineral exports, low investor confidence and limited foreign direct investment have all constrained job creation and wealth redistribution.

As the economy stabilized, domestic food production increased and shops restocked with food imported primarily from South Africa. Given the straitened circumstances of most urban households in 2008, there were grounds for optimism that post-crisis economic recovery and political stability might exercise a positive impact on urban food security in the country. However, political tensions continue to reduce the state's effectiveness in improving the everyday lives of most citizens, and particularly urban residents who wanted fundamental political reforms and grew increasingly disillusioned with the coalition government.[17] The 2013 election gave the ZANU-PF full control over government but subsequent policies have led to staple food supply problems, price increases, and vulnerability to changes in weather.[18] At the same time, formal and informal sector retailers have proliferated in Zimbabwe's cities and continue to re-shape urban food networks and consumption patterns.

The central question addressed in this report is whether food security in Zimbabwe's urban centres has improved since the height of the crisis. In other words, are positive macro-economic trends translating into ground-level improvements in incomes, poverty levels and food security? There is certainly an argument that little has changed for those at the bottom: problems of unemployment and low salaries have persisted. Most households face new challenges: the debt burden resulting from the unilateral conversion of household water, electricity and other municipal charges to the US dollar, high tariffs charged by local authorities, and the high costs of health and education services and transportation, which leave residents with little money to purchase food.[19] To try to answer this question, AFSUN conducted a follow-up household food security survey in Harare

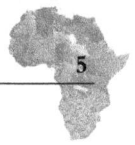

in 2012. The areas of the city surveyed and the survey instrument used were the same as in 2008, allowing for direct longitudinal comparisons of continuity and change. This report is structured along the same lines as the 2008 survey report and makes direct comparisons between the findings at these two points in time.

2. METHODOLOGY

The 2008 and 2012 surveys took place in the same three low-income neighbourhoods of Harare – Mabvuku, Tafara, and Dzivarasekwa. Mabvuku and Tafara are contiguous neighbourhoods established in the 1950s to accommodate black rural-to-urban migrant labourers on the eastern fringes of the city. Mabvuku and Tafara hosted many individuals and events associated with the anti-colonial movement in the twentieth century, and today the neighbourhood continues to be a centre for political resistance and activism. Dzivarasekwa was established later but serves a similar purpose in housing low-income families in high-density settlements. Within each of the selected neighbourhoods, participating households were randomly selected and household heads or their representatives were identified within each of these households for interview. A total of 351 households (with 1,517 individuals) were interviewed in the three study areas in 2012, lower than the 462 interviewed in 2008 but sufficient to make meaningful comparisons (Table 1). Enumerators from the University of Zimbabwe collected data from the households using the standardized AFSUN questionnaire. The questionnaire gathered information about household demographic characteristics, poverty data, income and expenditure patterns, household food security, food consumption patterns, and household coping mechanisms.

The mean household size in 2012 was 4.3, significantly lower than the mean of 5.6 in 2008 (Table 1). The largest household in 2008 had 16 members while the largest household in 2012 had 13. The proportion of households with 1-5 members increased from 56% in 2008 to 77% in 2012. On the other hand, the proportion of larger households with 6-10 members fell from 42% in 2008 to 22% in 2012. Extremely small households with one or two members were more prevalent in the 2012 sample (19%) than in 2008 (5%). Although the reasons for this apparently dramatic reshaping of household demography are open to speculation, the data on household type provides a possible clue.

FIGURE 1: Location of Study Areas in Harare

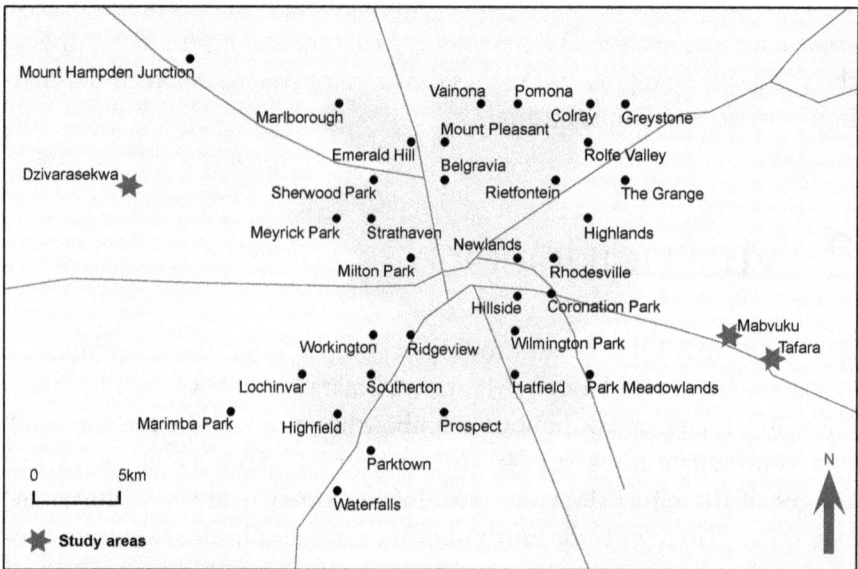

Source: Adapted from www.googlemaps.com

TABLE 1: Sample and Household Size

	2008	2012
Total number of households sampled	462	351
Total sample population	2,572	1,517
Average household size	5.6	4.3
Median household size	5.0	4.0
Smallest household size	1	1
Largest household size	16	13

The AFSUN survey questionnaire categorized households into four types based on the gender and relationships of the members. Female-centred households are headed by a woman without a partner and include any combination of immediate relatives (including her children, siblings, parents and grandparents). The proportion of female-centred households in the 2012 survey (24%) was almost the same as in 2008 (23%) (Table 2). Male-centred households are headed by a man without a partner and include any combination of immediate relatives (including his children, siblings, parents and grandparents). The proportion of male-headed households in 2012 (9%) was also very similar to 2008 (8%) (Table 2). Nuclear households include a head and a spouse or partner, with or without children, but without other relatives in the household. The proportion of nuclear households in 2012 was 44%, a slight increase from 37% in the 2008 survey (Table 2). Finally, extended households have a head, a spouse or partner, immediate relatives and a combination of other members (relatives and non-relatives). The proportion of extended households decreased from 32% in 2008 to 22% in 2012 (Table 2). One reason for the decline in overall household size therefore appears to be a decline in the number of extended family units, suggesting that at the height of the crisis taking in impoverished or destitute relatives may have been a coping strategy.

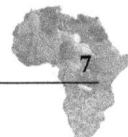

TABLE 2: Household Types in Surveyed Population				
	2008		2012	
	No.	%	No.	%
Female-centred	104	23	85	24
Male-centred	35	8	32	9
Nuclear	173	37	156	44
Extended	150	32	78	22

3. CHANGES IN EMPLOYMENT, INCOME AND EXPENDITURE

A comparison of the 2008 and 2012 employment profile of household members suggests little change in the labour market prospects of poor urban households in Harare. Overall employment was only slightly different in 2012 (59% employed) than it had been in 2008 (58% employed). Unemployment figures were also very similar (at 42% in 2008 and 40% in 2012). However, within each sub-category there were clear shifts. First, among the employed there was a move away from full-time towards part-time employment. The proportion of all working-age adults employed full-time fell from 43% to 35% between 2008 and 2012 and the proportion employed part-time increased from 15% to 24%. Second, among the unemployed, a higher proportion were looking for work in 2012 (19%) than in 2008 (15%), which might suggest a perception of improved employment opportunities or reflect a younger demographic likely to be more economically active.

TABLE 3: Work Status of Household Members Aged 18-65				
	2008		2012	
	No.	%	No.	%
Employed full-time	598	43	300	35
Employed part-time	208	15	207	24
Unemployed and looking for work	203	15	163	19
Unemployed and not looking for work	368	27	176	21
Total	1,377	100	846	100

Cross-checking these figures with other data proved problematical. Official census data does not differentiate between part-time and full-time employment, for example.[20] The 2012 Census, which counts all people over the age of 14, estimated that 17% of the population of Harare Province were not in the labour force.[21] This group included students, economically inactive homemakers, retirees, and people with disabilities. The group of labour force participants who were unemployed, corresponding to the AFSUN category of "unemployed and looking for work," was 14%. The remaining 69% of the adult population included formally and informally employed workers, piece workers, and seasonal workers. The Census report does not provide disaggregated statistics for workers in these vastly different working conditions. Unsurprisingly, the AFSUN survey in 2012 found much higher unemployment rates and higher rates of adults not participating in the labour force in low-income settlements than in the Census data for the provincial population as a whole.

Urban households worldwide reduce their vulnerability by drawing on multiple types of income sources rather than relying solely on paid employment.[22] Having a wider range of income sources means that if one source fails, for example through job loss or illness, the household has other sources to draw on to mitigate the consequences. In the context of Harare, multiple sources of income were necessary for a household to survive during the crisis of 2008 when the Zimbabwean dollar was almost worthless. In 2012, the pattern of multiple household income sources persisted even as income from wage work became relatively more prevalent. Despite the decline in the overall proportion of household members in full-time wage work between 2008 and 2012 (Table 3), the proportion of households receiving income from wage work actually increased from 55% in 2008 to 65% in 2012 (Table 4). And, despite the increase in the proportion of household members working part time, the proportion of households receiving income from casual work declined from 32% in 2008 to 24% in 2012 (Table 4).

The proportion of households deriving income from informal sector activity fell from 42% in 2008 to 34% in 2012, which does seem to indicate a small reduction in the importance of informality, which had become almost the only way for many households to survive in 2008. At the same time, the fact that one-third of all households were still obtaining income from informal activity in 2012 indicates that there has not been a massive decline in the importance of informal income sources for the urban poor (Table 4). The proportion of households receiving income from cash remittances was relatively low in 2008 and declined still further (from 12% to 6%) in 2012. In general, remittances have been shown to be a critical income source for urban and rural households in Zimbabwe over

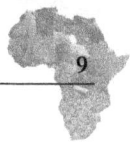

the last decade.[23] At the same time, the numbers of Zimbabweans leaving the country (and, in turn, remitting) have continued to rise.[24] What this data suggests is that poor urban households in Harare (from these communities at least) are largely excluded from the remitting economy.

The collapse of the Zimbabwean dollar, hyper-inflation, and the failure of many employers to provide salaries at the height of the crisis made it very difficult for household heads to estimate the income they received from each source in 2008. For this reason, the income data in Table 4, and the changes between 2008 and 2012, need to be treated with caution. In addition, the mean income from each source needs to be seen in relation to the percentage of households receiving income from that source; for example, even though the mean income of USD268 from formal business makes it a relatively lucrative source, only 3% of households received income this way (Table 4).

TABLE 4: Sources of Household Income and Mean Monthly Income from Each Source

	2008			2012		
	No.	% of house-holds	USD	No.	% of house-holds	USD
Wage work	253	55	77	229	65	440
Informal business	195	42	155	120	34	105
Casual work	150	32	95	83	24	138
Remittances	56	12	92	21	6	145
Rent	41	9	17	39	11	105
Formal business	14	3	268	6	2	227
Pension/disability allowance/grant	10	2	7	5	1	71
Sale of urban farm products	8	2	98	8	2	59
Sale of rural farm products	6	1	73	9	2	344
Gifts	6	1	19	16	5	96
Aid (money)	1	<1	6	0	0	N/A

Despite very high rates of formal sector unemployment, the most significant income source in both 2008 and 2012 was wage work. However, the average monetary value of this income source appears to have increased nearly sixfold from USD77 per month in 2008 to USD440 per month in 2012 (Table 4). This change suggests that there might have been an improvement in household purchasing power, although the value of income from the second most common income source, informal business, declined from USD155 per month in 2008 to USD105 per month in 2012. The declining significance of incomes from informal business is linked to the reduction of demand in the informal sector as the formal sector improved, police crackdowns on informal vending, and the decreased profit margins and elimination of the currency blackmarket in the informal sector.[25]

To better understand the impact of household income changes on poverty, it is important to examine concurrent changes in household expenditure. The proportion of households incurring certain types of expenditure – including food and groceries, housing, education and medical expenses – was virtually the same in 2008 and 2012 (Table 5). However, there were significant changes in other expenditure categories. For example, the proportion of households spending money on transportation increased from 36% to 68% and on fuel from 58% to 70%, a clear reflection of the country's fuel supply problems in 2008 and the subsequent availability by 2012. There was a decline in the percentage of households purchasing goods for resale (21% to 8%) consistent with the reduction in formal and informal business. Few households (4%) reported saving any money in 2008, a figure that increased to 15% in 2012, suggesting slightly greater disposable income and confidence in the financial system. On the other hand, the percentage of households incurring expenses on the servicing or repayment of debt increased threefold, from 3% to 9%, confirmation of the growing burden of debt facing some low-income households.

TABLE 5: Household Expenditures by Category and Mean Monthly Amount of Each Expense						
	2008			2012		
	No.	% of households	USD	No.	% of households	USD
Food and groceries	428	94	57	346	99	91
Housing	413	90	7	308	89	69
Utilities	411	90	3	320	91	46
Fuel	266	58	10	244	70	16
Education	263	58	5	202	58	43
Transportation	164	36	29	238	68	46
Medical expenses	120	26	7	105	30	21
Goods purchased to sell	98	21	136	28	8	158
Funeral costs	42	9	11	38	11	42
Remittances	30	6	13	26	7	22
Savings	20	4	87	51	15	137
Debt service/repayment	15	3	6	32	9	74
Home-based care	11	2	15	11	3	19
Insurance	7	1	3	34	10	17

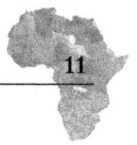

A focus on the changes in expenses incurred by each household suggests that life in Harare was far more costly in 2012 than in 2008, even with higher wage incomes. Expenditure in every category was higher in 2012, especially in housing, education, debt servicing/repayment (around 10 times as much), utilities (over 15 times the cost), and funeral costs (almost quadruple). Goods purchased to sell were the most costly expenditure item in both surveys (USD136 in 2008 and USD158 in 2012), dwarfing the incomes earned through informal and formal businesses and highlighting the financial risk incurred by households engaged in trading activities. Expenditure on food and groceries increased (but not as much as the cost of other basic necessities), rising from USD57 per month to USD91 per month (Table 5). Households are likely to have benefitted from more stable food prices that allowed them to plan for food expenses and maintain a tight budget where necessary. The sharp increase in expenditures on education is cause for concern that young people in low-income households will increasingly be marginalized from the more remunerative opportunities in the urban job market, thus reinforcing the intergenerational cycle of poverty.

4. HOUSEHOLD POVERTY

Income and expenditure data tell only part of the story of urban poverty in Harare in 2008 and 2012. Non-monetary livelihood strategies and transactions are obscured in these calculations even though they make up a large part of household economies, especially for the poor. This section reports on the participants' experiences of going without basic necessities, including food, as calculated in the Lived Poverty Index (LPI). The LPI score for each household is calculated on a scale of 0.0 to 4.0, whereby 0.0 represents the extreme of never going without and 4.0 the opposite extreme of always going without basic needs, including food to eat; clean water for home use; medicine or medical treatment; electricity in the home; fuel to cook food; and a cash income.

The mean LPI in Harare fell from 2.2 in 2008 to 1.6 in 2012. The quartile distribution of LPI scores shows a significant improvement in lived poverty in 2012, with the proportion of households in the least poor category increasing from 10% in 2008 to 28% in 2012 (Table 6). The proportion of households in the second least poor category also increased, from 35% in 2008 to 48% in 2012. The proportion of households in the lowest two quartiles correspondingly decreased from 55% in 2008 to 24% in 2012.

TABLE 6: Lived Poverty Index (LPI) Scores

	2008		2012	
	No.	%	No.	%
0-1 (never to seldom without)	42	10	96	28
1.01-2.00 (seldom to sometimes without)	152	35	162	48
2.01-3.00 (sometimes to often without)	193	45	73	22
3.01-4.00 (often to always without)	43	10	6	2
Total	430	100	337	100

The breakdown of "basic needs gone without" illustrates the changing dimensions of household poverty in Harare. Table 7 provides the responses to the questions used to calculate the LPI scores. Access to clean water and fuel for cooking improved but continued to be widespread problems in 2012. The proportion of households "many times/always" going without decreased significantly between 2008 and 2012 for clean water (67% to 37%), electricity (61% to 43%), medicine/medical treatment (40% to 14%) and cooking fuel (32% to 15%). At the same time, the proportion "never going without" clean water and electricity did not change significantly. The problem of clean water reflects a long-standing infrastructure deficit in Harare that is similar to many other Southern African cities.[26] The problem in Harare is exacerbated by concerns about water safety due to mismanagement of existing infrastructure and a lack of resources. The persistent problem with access to electricity is also caused by an infrastructure deficit and is directly related to the political and economic crisis. The improvement in access to medical treatment is the result of the improved conditions in 2012 for importing medicine with stable currencies.

The two LPI indicators most relevant to food security are having a cash income and enough food to eat. With regard to the former there was a clear improvement between 2008 and 2012. The proportion of households that "always/many times" went without a cash income declined from 59% to 31% and the proportion that "never went without" improved from 11% to 20%. Going without a cash income, even occasionally, means that households rely more on non-monetized livelihood activities, such as bartering, working for payment in kind, household production of basic needs (including urban agriculture), and drawing on social capital. In 2012, almost half (49%) of all households had gone without a cash income once or twice or several times in the previous year. The relative increase in the proportion of employed people working part-time probably indicates an increasing casualization of wage labour, with a greater likelihood of

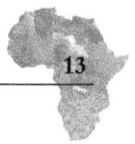

intermittent periods without a cash income in the household, even in a relatively stable macroeconomic context.

The proportion of households that "always/many times" went without enough food declined from 40% to 20% and the proportion that "never went without" improved from 19% to 25%. The LPI findings therefore suggest an overall improvement in incomes and food access although 55% still went without enough food. Even in the relatively stable economy of 2012, three-quarters of households had experienced food shortages in the previous year.

TABLE 7: Frequency of Going Without Basic Needs Over the Previous Year												
	Enough food to eat (% of households)		Clean water for home use (% of households)		Medicine or medical treatment (% of households)		Electricity in home (% of households)		Fuel to cook food (% of households)		A cash income (% of households)	
	2008	2012	2008	2012	2008	2012	2008	2012	2008	2012	2008	2012
Gone without many times/ always	40	20	67	37	40	14	61	43	32	15	59	31
Gone without once or twice/ several times	40	55	25	55	37	52	37	52	56	60	30	49
Never gone without	19	25	8	7	23	34	1	5	12	25	11	20

5. Shifting Sources of Food

Households in Harare access food from multiple sources, although patronage of various different types of food outlet shifted significantly between 2008 and 2012. In 2008, only 30% of households accessed food at supermarkets, whereas in 2012 the vast majority (92%) did (Figure 2). Increased use of supermarkets as a mainstream food source for the urban poor is consistent with the stabilization of the formal economy and the restocking of the empty shelves of 2008. Small shops and takeaways also increased dramatically in popularity, from being patronized by only 17% of households in 2008 to 73% of households in 2012. The increased patronage of supermarkets and small shops/takeaways did not appear to displace other food sources, however, but rather expanded the range of sources used. Informal markets/street food remained the most popular source, falling marginally from 97% of households in 2008 to 94% in 2012.

FIGURE 2: Household Food Sources

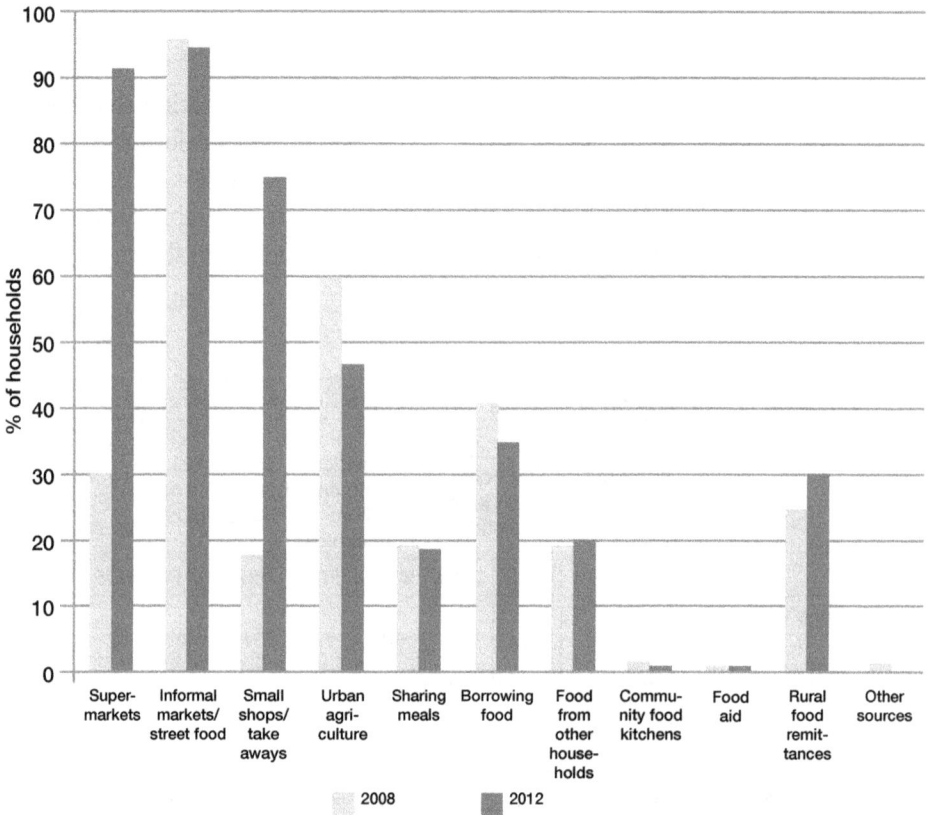

In both 2008 and 2012, supermarkets were most likely to be used on a monthly basis, in keeping with the frequency of wage and social grant payments (Figure 3). In contrast, informal markets were most likely to be used on a daily basis. Small shops/takeaways were also used more frequently than supermarkets, and the most common use pattern shifted from monthly in 2008 to daily in 2012. Supermarkets are still used less frequently in part because they are often located in formally planned areas at some distance from the informal areas surveyed.[27] Other advantages of informal markets and small shops/takeaways are that they are likely to facilitate price negotiation, offer flexibility in the quantity of food purchased, and provide informal credit arrangements.[28]

Urban agriculture has been a constant and expanding feature of the urban landscape in Harare since the early 1990s.[29] In recent years, urban agriculture has been associated primarily with low-income households with inadequate financial resources and insecure livelihood opportunities.[30] In both 2008 and 2012, very few households (around 2%) derived any income from the sale of home-grown produce. However, it has been and remains an important source of food for home consumption. The 2008 survey found that well over half (60%) of the households were engaged in urban agriculture as a food source (Figure 2). Furthermore, 70% of households producing their own food accessed it on at least a weekly basis (Figure 4). In 2012, the proportion of households reporting urban agriculture as a food source had declined from 60% to 46%, and 59% of these households used what they produced on at least a weekly basis. Although still very high by regional standards, urban agriculture appears to have declined in importance as purchased food has become more available. Another indication of this decline was evident in the responses to the question: "To what extent does the household *rely* on field crops and garden crops as additional livelihood strategies?" In the 2008 survey, 45% and 47% of households relied to some degree on garden crops and field crops respectively, whereas in 2012 these figures had fallen to 28% and 23% (Table 8). In other words, the proportion of households using urban agriculture to supplement food from other sources also fell. The reduction in the post-2008 importance of urban agriculture is not as sharp as one would expect if it was merely a short-term response to an acute economic crisis, however. Indeed, the continued importance of urban agriculture for many households after 2008 suggests it is an enduring part of urban lifestyles in Harare rather than a short-term response to unusually difficult circumstances.

FIGURE 3: Frequency of Patronage of Main Food Sources

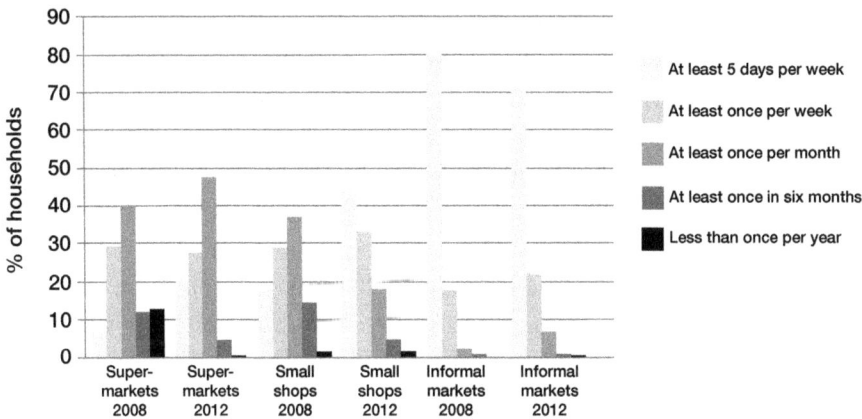

TABLE 8: Reliance on Urban Agricultural Livelihood Activities								
	Garden crops		Field crops		Livestock		Tree crops	
	2008	2012	2008	2012	2008	2012	2008	2012
Totally dependent	7	1	10	2	2	0	1	0
Partly dependent	20	11	23	13	3	<1	6	1
Slightly dependent	18	16	14	8	2	2	3	4
Not at all dependent	55	72	53	77	93	97	90	94

FIGURE 4: Frequency of Sourcing Food from Urban Agriculture

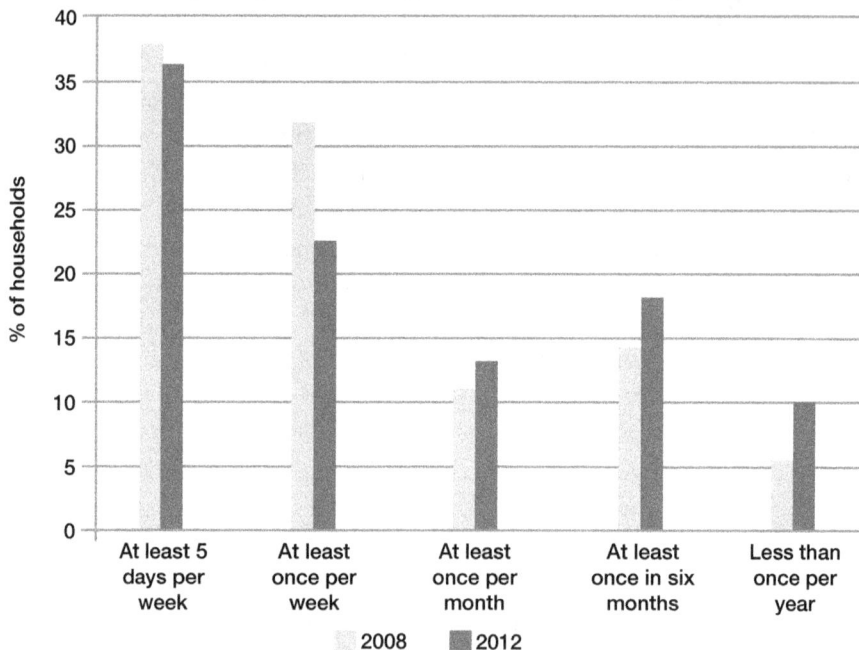

Food remittances from the countryside have received growing attention in urban food security research as an important non-monetized food source.[31] The proportion of households receiving food remittances increased slightly from 42% in 2008 to 47% in 2012 (Table 9). Most of this increase came from the rural areas (37% to 42%). Rural relatives remained the most important source of food remittances: 63% of recipient households in 2012, up from 55% in 2008. Although there is considerable controversy about the impact of the Fast Track Land Reform Programme on agriculture in Zimbabwe, there is an emerging consensus that resettled black farmers are producing a great deal more than they used to.[32] This could explain the continued and even increased flow of food remittances over time. Alternatively, the increase in 2012 may simply have reflected a better agricultural season in 2012. Other shifts between 2008 and 2012 included inter-urban food transfers with a slight drop in the proportion of households receiving food from other centres (from 43% to 37%).

Further insight into the changing nature of rural to urban food remittances can be gained through looking at the types of foodstuffs being remitted in 2008 and 2012. In 2008, the top three foods remitted (in terms of the proportion of recipient households) were cereals (95%), vegetables (35%), and foods made from beans, peas, lentils or nuts (30%) (Table 10). In 2012, the top three foods were cereals (80%), foods made from beans, peas, lentils, or nuts (39%), and fruits (24%). What is most striking is the decrease in remittances of vegetables (35% to 18%) and the simultaneous increase in remittances of fruit (5% to 24%) and roots and tubers (9% to 23%). The greater variety of foods remitted in 2012 could be a reflection of improved transportation linkages and better and more diverse agricultural production. The decline in cereals as a proportion of types of remittances could be indicative of improved urban maize markets in 2012. Food remittances continued to be seen as important in 2012, with half (49%) of remittance-receiving households saying they were very important or critical to survival, although this figure did drop from 83% in 2008 (Figure 5).

TABLE 9: Food Remittances from Rural and Urban Areas

Remitters	2008		2012	
	No.	% of recipient households	No.	% of recipient households
Rural relatives	105	55	103	63
Rural friends	19	10	12	7
Urban relatives	92	48	67	41
Urban friends	48	25	61	37
Geographical origin	No.	% of recipient households	No.	% of recipient households
Rural areas only	71	37	69	42
Urban areas only	82	43	60	37
Rural and urban areas	39	20	35	21
% of total households	192	42	164	47

Note: multiple response question

TABLE 10: Types of Foods Remitted to Urban Households from Rural Areas

	% of recipient households	
	2008	2012
Cereals (foods made from grain)	95	80
Roots or tubers	9	23
Vegetables	35	18
Fruits	5	24
Meat, poultry, or offal	6	10
Eggs	2	7
Fresh or dried fish or shellfish	1	8
Foods made from beans, peas, lentils, or nuts	30	39
Cheese, yoghurt, milk, or other milk products	6	4
Foods made with oil, fat, or butter	6	13
Sugar or honey	1	9
N	110	115

FIGURE 5: Importance of Food Remittances for Households

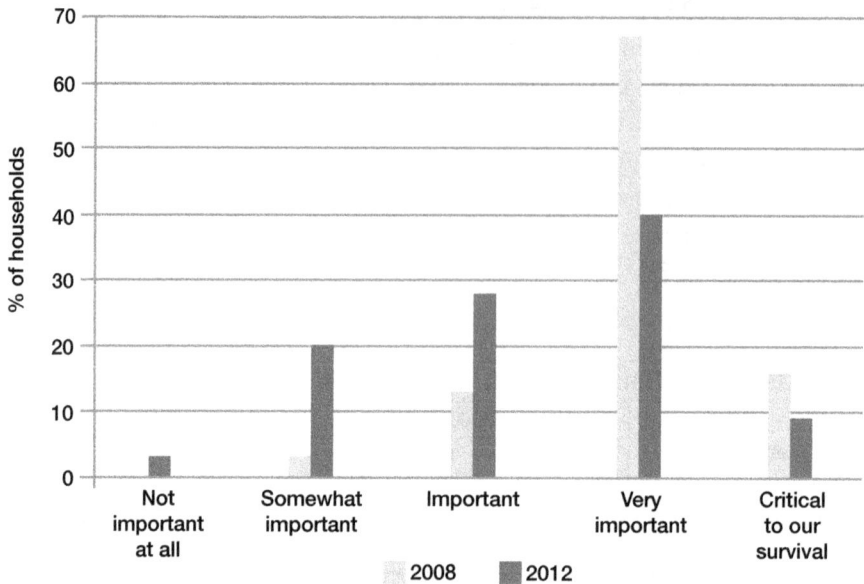

2008   2012

6. LEVELS OF FOOD INSECURITY

The AFSUN questionnaire measured food security levels using four international measurement tools developed by the Food and Nutrition Technical Assistance Project (FANTA):[33]

- Household Food Insecurity Access Score (HFIAS): The HFIAS measures the degree of food insecurity during the month prior to the survey. An HFIAS score is calculated for each household based on answers to nine "frequency-of occurrence" questions. The minimum score is 0 and the maximum is 27. The higher the score, the more food insecurity the household experienced.

- Household Food Insecurity Access Prevalence (HFIAP): The HFIAP indicator uses the responses to the HFIAS questions to group households into four levels of household food insecurity: food secure, mildly food insecure, moderately food insecure, and severely food insecure.

- Household Dietary Diversity Score (HDDS): Dietary diversity refers to how many food groups are consumed within the household in the previous 24 hours. The maximum number, based on the FAO classification of food groups for Africa, is 12. An increase in the average number of different food groups consumed provides a quantifiable measure of improved household food access.

- Months of Adequate Household Food Provisioning (MAHFP). This indicator captures changes in the household's ability to ensure that food is available above a minimum level the year round. Households are asked to identify in which months (during the past 12) they did not have access to sufficient food to meet their household needs.

In 2008, these areas of Harare had one of the worst HFIAS scores of all the low-income neighbourhoods in 11 cities surveyed by AFSUN (a mean of 14.7 and a median of 16.0) (Table 11). Only Manzini in Swaziland (a country ravaged by HIV and AIDS) had a higher mean (14.9) than Harare although its median score was lower (14.0). In 2012, both the mean and median scores in Harare were considerably lower (at 9.6 and 10.0 respectively). Scores like that in 2008 would have made it one of the less food insecure cities in the region (akin to Windhoek and Maputo but better than cities such as Gaborone, Lusaka and Cape Town).

TABLE 11: HFIAS Results in AFSUN Surveys			
	No. of households	Mean	Median
Harare (2012)	342	9.6	10.0
Harare (2008)	454	14.7	16.0
Windhoek	442	9.3	9.0
Gaborone	391	10.8	11.0
Maseru	795	12.8	13.0
Manzini	489	14.9	14.0
Maputo	389	10.4	10.0
Blantyre	431	5.3	4.0
Lusaka	386	11.5	11.0
Cape Town	1,026	10.7	11.0
Msunduzi	548	11.3	11.0
Johannesburg	976	4.7	1.5

The HFIAP scores provide further insight into the absolute and relative improvement in food security status in Harare between 2008 and 2012. In 2008, Harare had the lowest number of food secure households (2%) and the second highest number of severely food insecure households (72%). In 2012, the share of food secure households had increased to 10%; the share of mildly food insecure households increased from 3% to 7%; the share of moderately food insecure households decreased from 24% to 20%; and the proportion of severely food insecure households fell from 72% to 63% (Figure 6). Even with the drop in the mean and median HFIAS scores, the share of severely food insecure households remained alarmingly high in 2012. The discrepancy in the picture presented by changes in the HFIAS as opposed to the more incremental HFIAP redistribution is consistent with an argument that food security gains were accrued to a small group of households that benefitted from economic stabilization.

FIGURE 6: Distribution of Households in HFIAP Categories

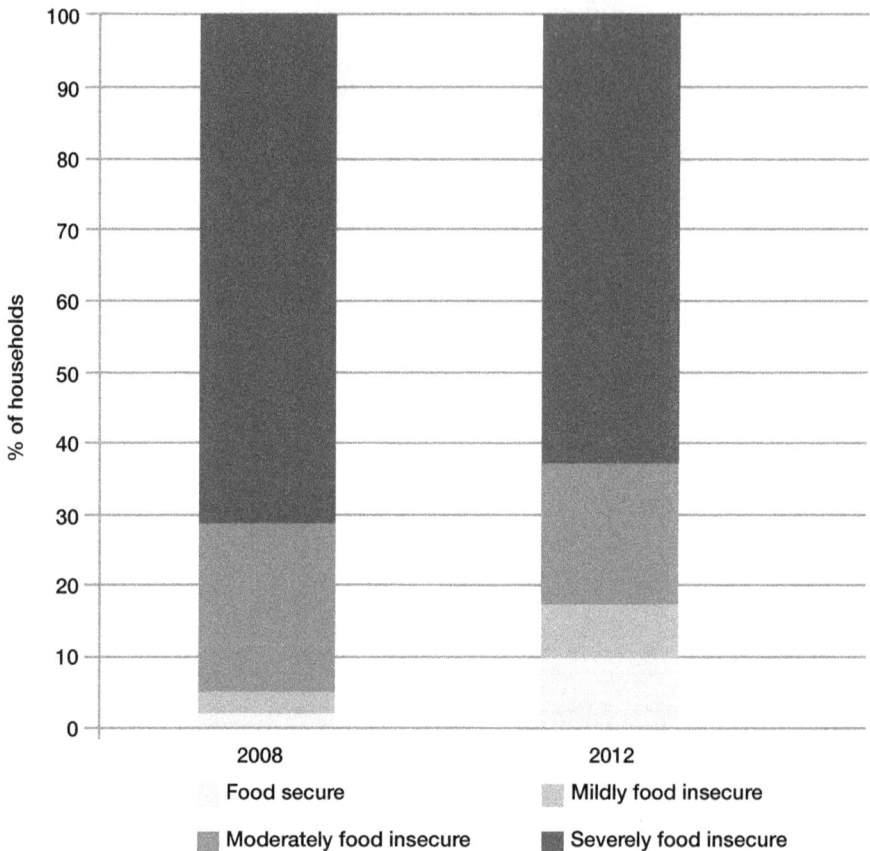

Food secure
Mildly food insecure
Moderately food insecure
Severely food insecure

Aggregate household dietary diversity also appears to have improved between 2008 and 2012. The HDDS rose from a mean score of 4.8 in 2008 to 6.5 in 2012. The median score improved from 5 in 2008 to 6 in 2012. A comparison of the distribution of HDDS scores at the two points in time shows a significant fall in the number of households with scores of 1-5 (Figure 7). Whereas nearly one-third (29%) of households in 2008 were in the extremely low range of 1-3, only 9% were in this category in 2012. Many more households were also at the high end of the scale in 2012, with 30% of households consuming foods from at least eight food groups on the day prior to the survey compared to only 12% in 2008.

The improvement in dietary diversity is reflected in the more widespread consumption of foods from almost every food group (Table 12). The only food group consumed by a lower proportion of households in 2012 than in 2008 was vegetables (consumed by 92% of households in 2008 and by 83% of households in 2012). The most substantial increases were in the consumption of dairy products (12% in 2008 and 39% in 2012), meat (22% in 2008 and 50% in 2012), fruits (15% in 2008 and 41% in 2012), and sugar or honey (64% in 2008 and 83% in 2012). With the arguable exception of increased fruit consumption, the foods with the sharpest increases conform to a more typical urban diet associated with the dietary transition taking place throughout the Global South.[34] Even as food becomes more abundant and accessible, the increased consumption of fatty, calorie-dense, and processed foods could be putting Harare on a more general path with negative impacts on health in the long term.

FIGURE 7: Distribution of Household Dietary Diversity Scores

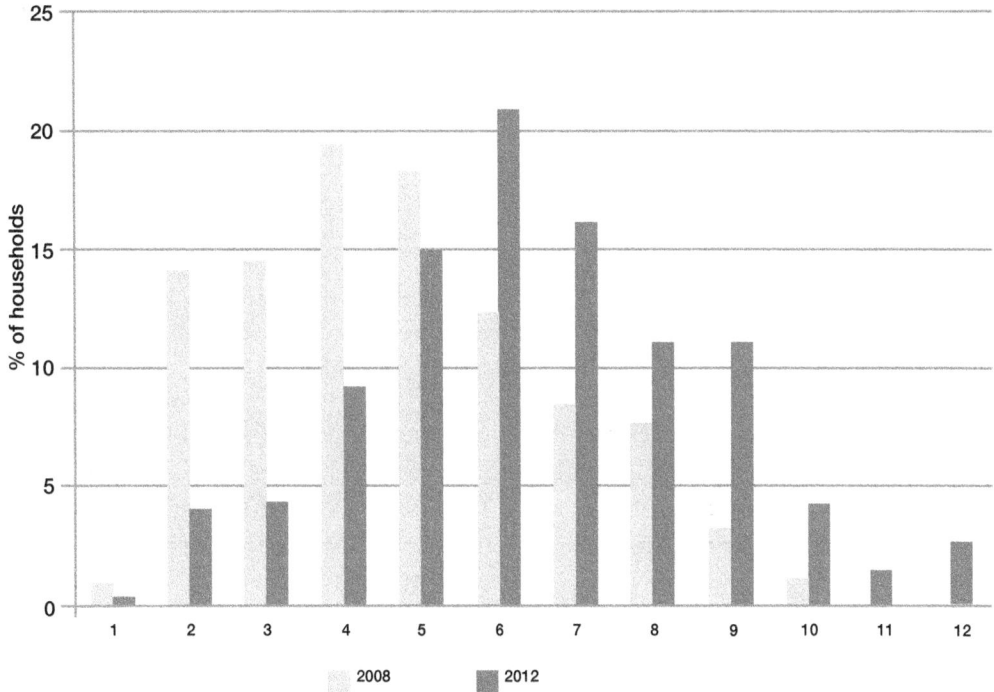

TABLE 12: Food Groups Consumed in Prior 24 Hours

	2008		2012	
	No.	%	No.	%
Cereals (foods made from grain)	455	99	344	98
Roots or tubers	57	12	109	31
Vegetables	423	92	293	83
Fruits	70	15	142	41
Meat, poultry, or offal	103	22	176	50
Eggs	40	9	75	21
Fresh or dried fish or shellfish	81	18	64	18
Foods made from beans, peas, lentils, or nuts	84	18	87	25
Cheese, yoghurt, milk, or other milk products	54	12	138	39
Foods made with oil, fat, or butter	261	56	255	73
Sugar or honey	295	64	292	83
Other foods	284	62	295	84

The fourth measurement tool for assessing household food security was the MAHFP. Fewer households experienced many months of inadequate food provisioning in the 2012 survey than in 2008 (Figure 8).

FIGURE 8: Distribution of MAHFP Scores

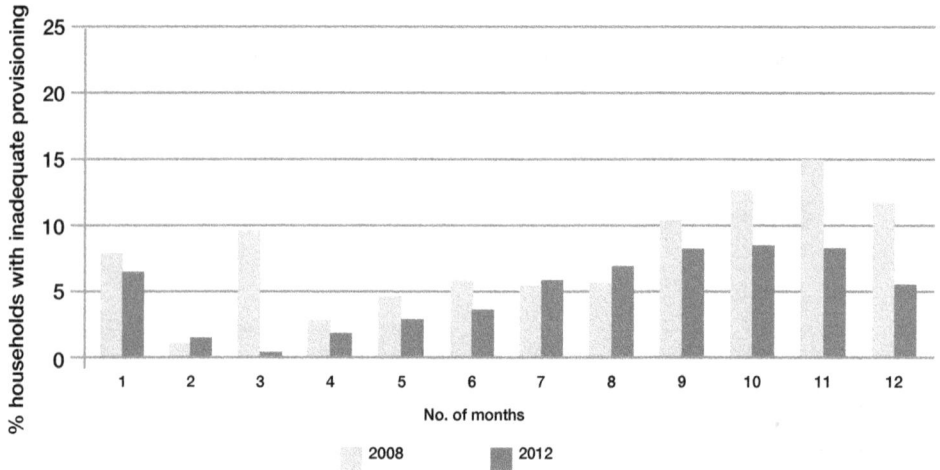

In 2008, September was the leanest month, during which three-quarters of households had inadequate food (Figure 9). November and December were the best months in the 2008 survey. In the 2012 survey, however, January was the most likely month for inadequate food provisioning and December was the least common month.

FIGURE 9: Proportion of Households with Inadequate Food Provisioning by Month

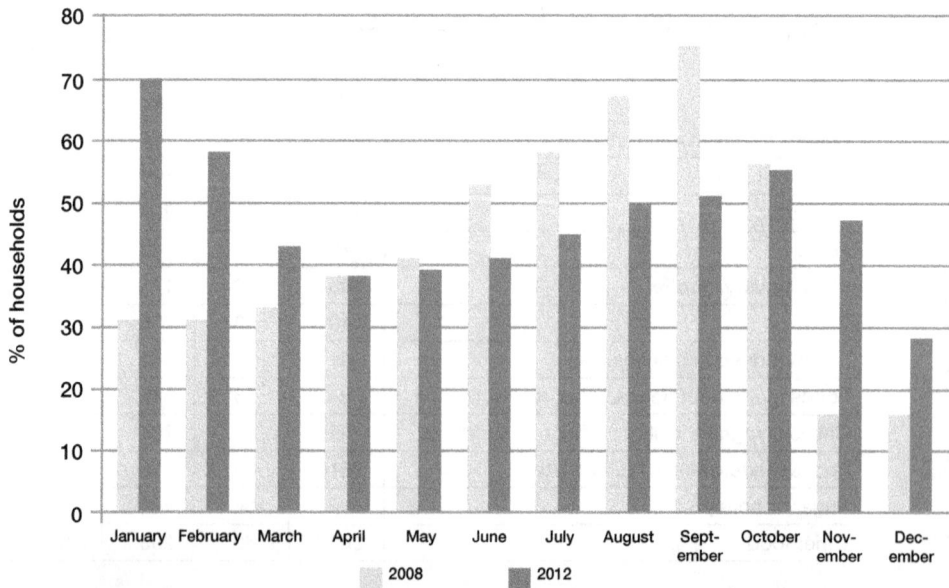

The marked change in seasonal pattern can partly be explained by the fact that in 2008, households were far more sensitive to the agricultural cycle where June-October is the dry season when little food is harvested. With people relying heavily on remittances and urban agriculture in 2008, it stands to reason that the harvest cycle contributed to September being the leanest month. The greater availability of food for purchase in 2012 meant that households were more able to smooth their consumption in the lean agricultural season. In addition, the emergence of January as the month with greatest food inadequacy is a reflection of a shift back to a long-standing pattern of overspending and overconsumption during December festivities.

7. Determinants of Variability in Food Security

While many factors contribute to food access, rapid price increases such as those experienced during the extraordinarily high inflation of 2008 force consumers to cut back on purchases, reduce food consumption, sacrifice nutritional value for sustenance, and make trade-offs between food and other basic needs. Respondents in both 2008 and 2012 were asked whether the household had gone without certain types of food because of prices over the previous six months. In 2008, a third of households (32%) experienced daily shortages due to food price increases (Figure 10). More than two-thirds experienced going without food on at least a weekly basis and only 4% never went without food. In 2012, the proportion experiencing daily shortages had declined from 32% to only 4%. On the other hand, the proportion of households that had never experienced shortages increased even more dramatically from 4% in 2008 to 51% in 2012 (Figure 10).

In 2008, the most common foods that people went without due to price increases were dairy products (84%), eggs (83%), meats, poultry, or offal (79%), and roots or tubers (78%) (Figure 11). These food types tend to be rich in protein, fats, and micronutrients, and omitting them from the diet on a consistent basis could have long-term health consequences, especially for children. Few households went without vegetables because of price increases, probably reflecting the importance of urban horticulture and the consistent availability of vegetables in the city. In 2012, those households that went without food due to price increases went without meat, poultry, or offal (83%), cereals (52%) and dairy products (54%).

FIGURE 10: Frequency of Going Without Food Due to Price Increases

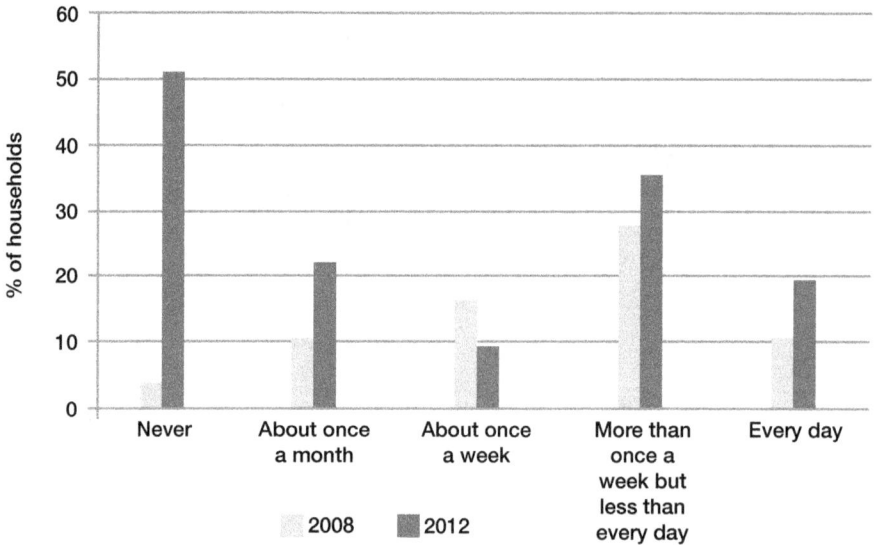

FIGURE 11: Types of Foods Not Consumed Due to Price Increases

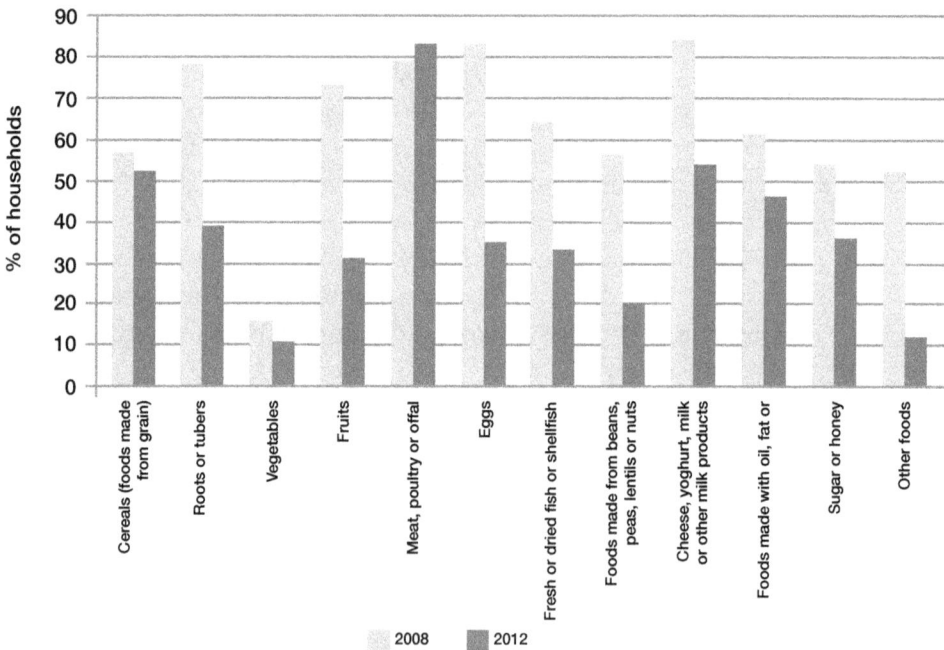

Most of the analysis in this report has dealt with households in the aggregate. However, by cross-tabulating household characteristics with mean food security scores, it is possible to determine which types of households were more or less food secure and how this changed between 2008 and 2012. Table 13 shows that there was an overall improvement in food security scores among all household size groups. However, the magnitude of the improvement did differ: for example, households with 1-5 members reduced their mean HFIAS by 4.7 and improved their HDDS and MAHFP by 1.7. The equivalent improvements for households with 6-10 members were 5.6 (HFIAS), 1.7 (HDDS) and 1.5 (MAHFP). In 2012 as in 2008, households with fewer members had lower HFIAS scores. The difference in mean HFIAS scores between households with 1-5 members and those with 6-10 members was therefore less in 2012 (0.9) than in 2008 (1.8), suggesting that additional household members were less challenging to feed in 2012.

The mean HDDS score for households with 1-5 members was higher than for households with 6-10 members by a consistent difference of 0.3. There was no difference in MAHFP scores for these two groups in 2008, but in 2012 smaller households had a slightly better MAHFP score (9.0) than medium-sized households (8.8) (Table 13). In all food insecurity scores, very large households consistently scored worse than smaller households, a reflection of the higher dependency ratios.

TABLE 13: Mean Food Insecurity Scores by Household Size, Type and LPI Score

Household size	HFIAS		HDDS		MAHFP	
	2008	2012	2008	2012	2008	2012
1-5	13.9	9.2	4.9	6.6	7.3	9.0
6-10	15.7	10.1	4.6	6.3	7.3	8.8
>10	17.7	14.8	4.0	4.2	5.0	7.0
Household type	HFIAS		HDDS		MAHFP	
	2008	2012	2008	2012	2008	2012
Female-centred	16.1	10.5	4.3	6.2	6.6	8.8
Male-centred	14.4	9.1	5.1	5.6	7.5	9.6
Nuclear	14.3	9.1	4.8	6.6	7.3	9.0
Extended	14.4	9.4	4.9	6.9	7.6	8.8
LPI score	HFIAS		HDDS		MAHFP	
	2008	2012	2008	2012	2008	2012
0.00-1.00	8.5	4.5	6.2	7.6	9.3	10.7
1.01-2.00	12.5	10.1	5.3	6.1	8.2	8.9
2.01-3.00	17.1	14.1	4.2	5.7	6.4	6.6
3.01-4.00	18.9	16.0	4.0	4.8	6.1	9.5

In 2008, and in 2012, female-centred households were the least food secure type of household. There was a smaller gap between the HFIAS of nuclear and female-centred households in 2012 (1.4) than in 2008 (1.8), suggesting a relatively greater improvement for female-centred households (Table 13). The difference between female-centred and extended households closed even more, from 1.7 in 2008 to 1.1 in 2012, reflecting a worse position for extended households relative to other household types in 2012. The relatively worse position for extended households, which by definition have more members, seems to contradict the observation that being a household with more members was relatively less detrimental to household food security status in 2012. Nonetheless, it bears noting that many female-centred and nuclear households also have more than five members.

Female-centred households improved slightly more relative to nuclear households in terms of the HDDS, with a difference of 0.5 in 2008 and 0.4 in 2012 (Table 13). Male-centred households improved the least in terms of HDDS, falling from the highest mean score in 2008 to the lowest mean score in 2012 among household types. Male-centred households are the least common type and it is therefore difficult to generalize from these small numbers, but it is reasonable to expect that single men prepare for themselves a narrower set of meals, or possibly eat more at restaurants with a narrow selection of foods. Extended households had the highest mean HDDS in 2012 (Table 13). The difference in MAHFP scores among household types in 2012 was less than in 2008, with female-centred and male-centred households improving their scores relative to nuclear and extended households. Extended households improved the least in terms of MAHFP (difference of 1.2), while female-centred households showed the most improvement (difference of 2.2). Household type is intertwined with issues of gender and poverty and the relatively high food insecurity scores for female-centred households in 2008 and 2012 reflect the link between gender and poverty in Southern African cities. The closing of the food security gap between female-centred and other household types suggests that single women with dependants were more severely affected than men and married women by the economic crisis.

Lower LPI scores were correlated with better food security scores in both surveys and by all measures of food security status. The single exception was the higher MAHFP score in 2012 for households with an LPI score of 3.01-4.00 than for households with LPI scores of 2.01-3.00 (Table 13). This was an anomaly due to the extremely small number of households with LPI scores above 3.01 in 2012 (only 2% of households surveyed). There was a wider difference in the mean HFIAS of the least poor and the second least poor group in 2012 (5.6) than in 2008 (4.0), and less of a difference between the two middle groups in 2012 (4.0) than in 2008 (4.6). HDDS was also relatively much better for the least poor households than the second least poor households in 2012 than in 2008 (difference of 1.5 rather than 0.9). The gap in HDDS between households with LPI scores of 1.01-2.00 and households with LPI scores of 2.01-3.00 was less in 2012 (0.4) than in 2008 (1.1).

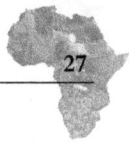

Cross-tabulating the food insecurity scores with the use of selected food sources by the households revealed further trends. In 2008, households that received food remittances from the rural areas had a lower mean HFIAS (13.6) than households that did not receive these remittances (14.8) (Table 14). In 2012, the opposite was true and households that received remittances had a higher mean HFIAS (10.1) than households that did not (9.7). This finding is consistent with the "importance of remittances for survival" finding (Figure 5), with remittances evidently playing a more important role in reducing the food insecurity of households that received them in 2008. There was little change in the relative difference in HDDS or MAHFP between these groups of households in 2008 and 2012 (Table 14).

TABLE 14: Mean Food Insecurity Scores by Selected Food Sources						
Food from rural remittances?	HFIAS		HDDS		MAHFP	
	2008	2012	2008	2012	2008	2012
Yes	13.6	10.1	5.2	6.8	7.5	9.2
No	14.8	9.7	4.7	6.4	7.2	8.9
Food from urban agriculture?	HFIAS		HDDS		MAHFP	
	2008	2012	2008	2012	2008	2012
Yes	14.8	9.3	4.7	6.5	7.3	8.9
No	14.2	10.1	4.8	6.4	7.1	9.0

The opposite trend appeared in cross-tabulations of household food insecurity indicators with households that grew some of their own food and those that did not. In 2008, households that reported growing their own food as a food source had a mean HFIAS of 14.8, which was higher than the mean HFIAS among households that never produced their own food (14.2) (Table 14). In 2012, this relationship was inverted and the households that did not produce any of their own food had a higher HFIAS (10.1) than those that produced some of their own food (9.3). One possible explanation for this trend is that many vulnerable households that do not normally produce their own food and, as a result, lack the necessary tools, inputs, and knowledge of agriculture, were engaging in subsistence food production during the crisis. The proportion of households engaging in urban agriculture in 2008 suggests that many vulnerable households were turning to this source as a coping mechanism, temporarily raising the food insecurity score for households engaged in urban agriculture relative to other households. The relatively positive score for households engaged in urban agriculture in 2012 suggests that these are households that normally produce their own food, not only in times of acute crisis. For these households, urban agriculture appears to have a positive impact on their food security status. As with rural remittances, there were negligible differences in the HDDS and MAHFP scores between these categories of households.

The cross-tabulation of household food insecurity scores with income terciles shows a remarkable consistency in the differences by group in 2008 and 2012 for all food insecurity scores (Table 15). The strong correlation between income level and food security status is consistent with other AFSUN surveys.[35] The type of income is also shown to have a significant impact on the food security scores, and the gap in HFIAS between households with a wage income source and without a wage income source widened from 0.4 in 2008 to 2.8 in 2012 (Table 15). The gap in terms of HDDS (from 0.2 in 2008 to 0.7 in 2012) and MAHFP (from 0.1 to 1.6) also widened, as households with a wage income benefitted much more from improvements in food security than households without a wage income. These findings provide further evidence to the observation that improvements in household food security in 2012 relative to 2008 were much greater for a small group of people. The economies of households receiving a wage income are more directly connected to the formal food economy, and policies directed at currency stabilization, food price stabilization through food imports, and the development of supermarkets are more likely to benefit this group.

TABLE 15: Mean Food Insecurity Scores by Income Level and Income from Wages

Income	HFIAS		HDDS		MAHFP	
	2008	2012	2008	2012	2008	2012
Lowest income	16.9	12.9	3.9	5.5	6.5	7.3
Middle income	14.2	10.1	4.8	6.3	7.3	8.9
Highest income	13.3	7.2	5.3	7.3	7.7	10.2
Income from wage work?	HFIAS		HDDS		MAHFP	
	2008	2012	2008	2012	2008	2012
Yes	14.4	8.7	4.9	6.7	7.3	9.5
No	14.8	11.5	4.7	6.0	7.2	7.9

8. CONCLUSION

The status of household food security in low-income neighbourhoods in Harare improved in 2012 relative to 2008, and yet persistently high rates of severe food insecurity demonstrate that the daily need to access adequate food continued to be a major challenge for most households. The stabilization of the formal economy by 2012 shaped household food

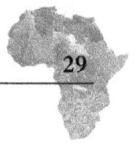

access in some key ways: more households received income from wage work, wage income was higher, and supermarkets and small shops were much more important food sources than they were in 2008 (although alternative food sources remained important). Most households continued to rely on a diverse set of livelihood and food security strategies even under these improved economic conditions, drawing on non-monetary informal food sources such as rural remittances and urban agriculture in consistently high numbers. Food price increases were less of a problem in 2012 than in 2008, but they continued to impede many households from accessing food on a regular basis.

The findings reported here suggest that improvements in food security status have accrued mostly to the least poor households. More households fell into the least poor category in 2012, suggesting a combination of two scenarios: households becoming less poor while also becoming less food insecure, and households that were already in the least poor category in 2008 that had higher food security scores in 2012. Because the survey did not track the same households, these trends represent a general widening of the food security gap in keeping with a widening poverty gap in low-income urban communities.

Many more households were in the least poor category in 2012, which appears to be the main factor that led them to be more food secure. The poorest categories of households were less food insecure in 2012 than in 2008, but they were more food insecure *relative to* the least poor households. These trends show that food security status in Harare is inextricably linked to other dimensions of poverty and that, even within low-income neighbourhoods, there is a wide differentiation in poverty rates and food security status among households. The key lesson for policy-makers is that even in the context of overall economic improvement, food insecurity remains endemic among the poorest segments of the urban population. Households are already accustomed to drawing on resources outside of the formal economy and improvements in employment income have not reversed that trend. These alternative livelihood strategies should therefore be considered as a normal part of urban life and supported with state resources that can improve access to food for the most marginalized groups and ensure the environmental sustainability of activities such as urban agriculture.

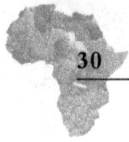

ENDNOTES

1   Quoted in J. Moyo, "Starvation Strikes Zimbabwe's Urban Dwellers" *Inter Press Service* 24 July 2015.

2   R. Howard-Hassmann, "Mugabe's Zimbabwe, 2000-2009: Massive Human Rights Violations and the Failure to Protect" *Human Rights Quarterly* 32(2010): 898-920; FEWSNET, *Zimbabwe Food Security Alert*, 24 September 2008.

3   J. Crush and D. Tevera (eds.), *Zimbabwe's Exodus: Crisis, Migration, Survival* (Ottawa: IDRC); D. Potts, *Circular Migration in Zimbabwe & Contemporary Sub-Saharan Africa* (Woodbridge, UK: James Currey, 2010); Government of Zimbabwe and the United Nations, *Zimbabwe 2012 Millennium Development Goals Progress Report* (Harare, 2012); J. McGregor and R. Primorac (eds.), *Zimbabwe's New Diaspora: Displacement and the Cultural Politics of Survival* (New York: Berghahn, 2010).

4   G. Tawodzera, L. Zanamwe, and J. Crush, *The State of Food Insecurity in Harare, Zimbabwe*. AFSUN Urban Food Security Series No. 13, Cape Town, 2012.

5   H. Besada and N. Moyo, "Zimbabwe in Crisis: Mugabe's Policies and Failures" CIGI Working Paper No 38, Waterloo, 2008; B. Raftopolous, "The Crisis in Zimbabwe, 1998-2008" In B. Raftopolous and A. Mlambo (eds.), *Becoming Zimbabwe: A History from the Pre-Colonial Period to 2008* (Harare: Weaver, 2009), pp. 201-32; S. Chiumbu and M. Musemwa (eds.), *Crisis! What Crisis?: The Multiple Dimensions of the Zimbabwean Crisis* (Cape Town: HSRC, 2012); J. Alexander and J. McGregor, "Introduction: Politics, Patronage and Violence in Zimbabwe" *Journal of Southern African Studies* 39(2013): 749-63.

6   J. Coomer and T. Gstraunthaler, "The Hyperinflation in Zimbabwe" *Quarterly Journal of Austrian Economics* 14(2011); 311-46.

7   D. Potts, "Making a Livelihood in (and Beyond) the African City: The Experience of Zimbabwe" *Africa* 81(2011): 588-605.

8   J. Muzondidya, "From Buoyancy to Crisis, 1980-1997" In Mlambo and Raftopolous, *Becoming Zimbabwe*.

9   P. Carmody, " Neoclassical Practice and the Collapse of Industry in Zimbabwe: The cases of Textiles, Clothing, and Footwear" *Economic Geography* 74(1998): 319-43; D. Potts and C. Mutambirwa, "'Basics are Now A Luxury': Perceptions of Structural Adjustment's Impact on Rural and Urban Areas in Zimbabwe" *Environment and Urbanization* 10(1998): 55-76; R. Chattopadhyay, "Zimbabwe: Structural Adjustment, Destitution and Food Insecurity" *Review of African Political Economy* 27(2000): 307-16.

10   I. Scoones, N. Marongwe, B. Mavedzenge, J. Mahenehene, F. Murimbarimba and F.Sulume, *Zimbabwe's Land Reform: Myths and Realities* (Harare: Weaver Press, 2010); P. Matondi, *Zimbabwe's Fast Track Land Reform* (London: Zed Books, 2012).

11   D. Potts, "'Restoring Order'? Operation Murambatsvina and the Urban Crisis in Zimbabwe" *Journal of Southern African Studies* 32(2006): 273-91; M. Vambe (Ed.), *The Hidden Dimensions of Operation Murambatsvina in Zimbabwe* (Harare: Weaver Press, 2010).

12   R. Newfarmer and M. Pierola, *Trade in Zimbabwe Changing Incentives to Enhance Competitiveness* (Washington DC: World Bank, 2015), p. 11; see also B. Kaminski and F. Ng, *Zimbabwe's Foreign Trade Performance during the Decade of Economic Turmoil* (Washington DC: World Bank, 2011).

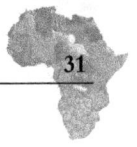

13   Zanamwe, Tawodzera and Crush, *The State of Food Security in Harare*; see also
      G. Tawodzera, "Vulnerability in Crisis: Urban Household Food Insecurity in
      Epworth, Harare, Zimbabwe" *Food Security* 3(2011): 503-520; G. Tawodzera,
      "Household Survival and Resilience to Food Insecurity in Crisis Conditions:
      The Case of Epworth in Harare, Zimbabwe" *Journal of Hunger and Environmental
      Nutrition* 7 (2-3) (2012): 293-320; G. Tawodzera, "Rural-Urban Transfers
      and Household Food Security in Harare's Crisis Context" *Journal of Food and
      Nutritional Disorders* (2013): 2-5; G. Tawodzera, "Household Food Insecurity and
      Survival: 2008 and Beyond" *Urban Forum* 25(2014): 207-216

14   J. Noko, "Dollarization: The Case of Zimbabwe" *Cato Journal* 31(2011): 339-65.

15   Newfarmer and Pierola, *Trade in Zimbabwe*, p 2.

16   Ibid., p. 32.

17   B. Magure, "Interpreting Urban Informality in Chegutu, Zimbabwe" *Journal
      of Asian and African Studies* (published online June 10, 2014); J. McGregor,
      "Surveillance and the City: Patronage, Power-Sharing and the Politics of Urban
      Control in Zimbabwe" *Journal of Southern African Studies* 39(2013): 783-805; S.
      Wilkins, "Ndira's Wake: Politics, Memory and Mobility among the Youth of
      Mabvuku-Tafara, Harare" *Journal of Southern African Studies* 39(2013): 885-901;
      F. Musoni, "Operation Murambatsvina and the Politics of Street Vendors in
      Zimbabwe" *Journal of Southern African Studies* 36(2010): 301-317.

18   B. Raftopolous, "The 2013 Elections in Zimbabwe: The End of an Era" *Journal of
      Southern African Studies* 39(2013): 971-88

19   J. Manjengwa, S. Feresu and A. Chimhowu, "Understanding Poverty, Promoting
      Wellbeing and Sustainable Development: A Sample Survey of 16 Districts of
      Zimbabwe" Institute of Environmental Studies, University of Zimbabwe, Harare,
      2012.

20   Zimbabwe National Statistics Agency, *Zimbabwe Population Census Report 2012:
      Harare Provincial Report* (Harare, 2013), p. 70.

21   Ibid.

22   C. Rakodi and T. Lloyd-Jones (eds.), *Urban Livelihoods: A People-Centred Approach
      to Reducing Poverty*. (London: Earthscan, 2002).

23   S. Bracking and L. Sachikonye, "Migrant Remittances and Household Wellbeing
      in Urban Zimbabwe" *International Migration* 48(5) (2010): 203–27; D. Tevera,
      J. Crush and A. Chikanda, "Migrant Remittances and Household Survival in
      Zimbabwe" In Crush and Tevera, *Zimbabwe's Exodus*, pp. 307-23; T. Mukwedeva,
      "Zimbabwe's Saving Grace: The Role of Remittances in Household Livelihood
      Strategies in Glen Norah, Harare" *South African Review of Sociology* 42(1) (2011):
      116-30. D. Makina, "Migration and Characteristics of Remittance Senders in
      South Africa" *International Migration* 51(2013): e148-e158.

24   Crush and Tevera, *Zimbabwe's Exodus*.

25   A. Makochekanwa, "Zimbabwe's Black Market for Foreign Exchange" Working
      Paper No. 13, Department of Economics, University of Pretoria, 2007; T. Chirau
      and P. Chamuka, "Politicisation of Urban Space: Evidence from Women Informal
      Traders at Magaba, Harare in Zimbabwe" *Global Advanced Research Journal of
      History, Political Science and International Relations* 2 (2013): 14-26.

26   G. Ruiters, "Social Control and Social Welfare Under Neoliberalism in South
      African Cities: Contradictions in Free Basic Water Services." In M. Murray and

G. Myers (eds.), *Cities in Contemporary Africa* (New York: Palgrave MacMillan, 2006), pp. 289-318; M. Musemwa, "From 'Sunshine City' to a Landscape of Disaster: The Politics of Water, Sanitation and Disease in Harare, Zimbabwe, 1980–2009" *Journal of Developing Societies* 26 (2010): 165-206; E. Manzungu and R. Chioreso, "Internalising a Crisis? Household Level Response to Water Scarcity in the City of Harare, Zimbabwe" *Journal of Social Development in Africa* 27 (2012).

27   J. Crush and B. Frayne, "Supermarket Expansion and the Informal Food Economy in Southern African Cities: Implications for Urban Food Security" *Journal of Southern African Studies* 37(2011): 781-807.

28   R. Mupedziswa, and P. Gumbo, *Women Informal Traders in Harare and the Struggle for Survival in an Environment of Economic Reform.* (Uppsala: Nordiska Afrikainstitutet, 2001). I. Chrisa, "Post-2005 Harare: A Case of the Informal Sector and Street Vending Resilience: What Options Do Key Actors Have?" *Local Governance Development Journal* 1(2007); H. Tamukamoyo, "Survival in a Collapsing Economy: A Case Study of Informal Trading at a Zimbabwean Flea Market" PhD thesis, University of the Witwatersrand, Johannesburg, 2009; G. Dube, "A Study of the Self-Employed in the Urban Informal Sector in Harare" MA thesis, University of KwaZulu-Natal, Durban, 2010; J. Jones, "'Nothing is Straight in Zimbabwe': The Rise of the *Kukiya-kiya* Economy 2000-2008" *Journal of Southern African Studies* 36(2010): 285-99; A. Weston, "Creativity in the Informal Economy of Zimbabwe" PhD thesis, Kingston, London, 2012.

29   D. Drakakis-Smith, "Food Systems and the Poor in Harare Under Conditions of Structural Adjustment" *Geografiska Annaler. Series B, Human Geography* 76(1994): 3-20; D. Drakakis-Smith, T. Bowyer-Bower, and D. Tevera, D. "Urban Poverty and Urban Agriculture: An Overview of Linkages in Harare" *Habitat International* 19(1995): 183-193; B. Mbiba, "Classification and Description of Urban Agriculture in Harare" *Development Southern Africa* 12(l) (1995): 75-86; D. Tevera, "Urban Agriculture in Africa: A Comparative Analysis of Findings from Zimbabwe, Kenya and Zambia" *African Urban Quarterly* 11(2/3) (1999): 181-7.

30   C. Mutonodzo, "The Social and Economic Implications of Urban Agriculture on Food Security in Harare, Zimbabwe" In M. Redwood (ed.), *Agriculture in Urban Planning: Generating Livelihoods and Food Security* (London and Ottawa: Earthscan and IDRC, 2009), pp. 73-89; P. Toriro, "Gender Dynamics in the Musikavanhu Urban Agriculture Movement, Harare, Zimbabwe" In A. Hovorka, H. de Zeeuw and M. Njenga (eds.), *Women Feeding Cities: Mainstreaming Gender in Urban Agriculture and Food Security* (Rugby: Practical Action Publishing, 2009), pp. 93-104.

31   B. Frayne, "Pathways of Food: Mobility and Food Transfers in Southern African Cities" *International Development Planning Review* 32(2010): 291-310; A. Andersson, "Maize Remittances, Smallholder Livelihoods and Maize Consumption in Malawi" *Journal of Modern African Studies* 49(2011): 1-25.

32   J. Hanlon, J. Manjengwa and T. Smart, *Zimbabwe Takes Back Its Land* (Sterling, Virginia: Kumarian Press, 2012).

33   J. Coates, A. Swindale, and P. Bilinsky, "Household Food Insecurity Access Scale (HFIAS) for Measurement of Household Food Access: Indicator Guide (Version 3)" *Food and Nutrition Technical Assistance Project* (Washington, DC: Academy for Educational Development, 2007); A. Swindale and P. Bilinsky, "Household Dietary Diversity Score (HDDS) for Measurement of Household Food Access: Indicator Guide (Version 2)" *Food and Nutrition Technical Assistance Project*

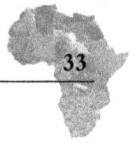

(Washington, DC: Academy for Educational Development, 2006); P. Bilinsky and A. Swindale, "Months of Adequate Household Food Provisioning (MAHFP) for Measurement of Household Food Access: Indicator Guide" Food and Nutrition Technical Assistance Project (Washington, DC: Academy for Educational Development, 2007).

34 J. Crush, B. Frayne, and M. McLachlan, *Rapid Urbanization and the Nutrition Transition in Southern Africa*. AFSUN Urban Food Security Series No. 7, Cape Town, 2011.

35 B. Frayne et al., *The State of Urban Food Insecurity in Southern Africa*. AFSUN Urban Food Security Series No. 2, Cape Town, 2010.

www.ingramcontent.com/pod-product-compliance
Lightning Source LLC
Chambersburg PA
CBHW080648270326
41928CB00017B/3231